TATTOO ART

by Ryan Gale

BrightP◆int Press

San Diego, CA

BrightPoint Press

© 2022 BrightPoint Press
an imprint of ReferencePoint Press, Inc.
Printed in the United States

For more information, contact:
BrightPoint Press
PO Box 27779
San Diego, CA 92198
www.BrightPointPress.com

LIBRARY OF CONGRESS CATALOGING-IN-PUBLICATION DATA

Names: Gale, Ryan, author.
Title: Tattoo art / by Ryan Gale.
Description: San Diego, CA : BrightPoint Press, [2022] | Series: Exploring art | Includes
   bibliographical references and index. | Audience: Grades 7-9
Identifiers: LCCN 2021005756 (print) | LCCN 2021005757 (eBook) | ISBN 9781678201241
   (hardcover) | ISBN 9781678201258 (eBook)
Subjects: LCSH: Tattooing--Juvenile literature.
Classification: LCC GT2345 .G35 2022 (print) | LCC GT2345 (eBook) | DDC 391.6/5--dc23
LC record available at https://lccn.loc.gov/2021005756
LC ebook record available at https://lccn.loc.gov/2021005757

CONTENTS

AT A GLANCE

- Tattoo art modifies the body. It is made when someone inserts pigments into skin. This makes the art permanent.

- The term *tattoo* comes from the Samoan word *tatau*. Samoa is an island nation in the Pacific Ocean.

- Tattoo art has been around for thousands of years. The oldest example was found on a 5,300-year-old mummy discovered in Europe.

- Some researchers think ancient people may have gotten tattoos as a medical treatment to help relieve pain.

- In some cultures, tattoo art was believed to ward off evil. In others, it was used to show a person's achievements and family history. Some used tattooing as a form of punishment.

- A college degree is not necessary to become a tattoo artist. Most people learn by training with other artists. It can take years of training and practice to become a good tattoo artist.

- Scientists are helping to bring about new tattoo art styles. They are creating new types of ink that glow in the dark and change color.

A HUMAN CANVAS

Daniel sat in a chair in a brightly lit room. A tattoo artist leaned close to him. She carefully outlined an image on his arm with an electric tattoo machine. Daniel thought the machine's vibrating needles sounded like a swarm of bees. He also thought the needles felt like bees stinging his arm. But he had to keep his

Many tattoo artists have tattoos of their own.

arm perfectly still even though it hurt. If he

moved, the artist could make a mistake.

This was Daniel's first tattoo. He wanted

it to look perfect. He knew the pain was

only temporary, and the artwork on his arm would last forever.

TATTOOING THE BODY

Millions of people have tattoo art. Tattoo art can make a person look unique. This art form has been around for thousands of years. The word *tattoo* comes from the Samoan word *tatau*. It means "to mark."[1] The island of Samoa is in the southern Pacific Ocean.

Tattoo art is found around the world. Some **cultures** learned about tattooing from other cultures, while some developed

People can get colored or black-and-white tattoos. Some people have both kinds on their bodies.

it on their own. Each culture created its own

unique style of tattoo art.

People get tattoo art for many reasons. Some people want to show pride in their cultures. Others may believe the images will bring them luck or protection. Some people use tattoo art to cover scars, while others use it to express themselves. Painters use canvases to paint on. Some people see their bodies as canvases. They want to cover their bodies with art.

There are some people who do not approve of tattoo art. They may see tattoo art as disfiguring the body. Tattoo art has also been linked with criminals in the past. Some people still think only bad people

People can get tattoos on many different parts of the body.

get tattoos. These views have kept tattoo art from being more widely accepted. But its popularity continues to grow as more people gain interest.

CHAPTER ONE

WHAT IS TATTOO ART?

Tattoo art is a type of body modification. Body modification is the permanent altering of the body. Other types of this modification can include piercing and scarring. Tattoo art involves decorating the body with images and words. The tattooing process puts **pigments** into a person's skin. This makes the tattoo permanent.

Some people get both piercings and tattoos.

THE SCIENCE OF TATTOO ART

Most tattoo art is made by a tattoo artist.

He or she inserts ink under a person's skin.

The artist does this by piercing the skin with

small, metal needles. A tattoo artist dips

the needles into a container of ink. The ink clings between the tips of the needles, like paint on a paintbrush. When the needles are inserted into the skin, the ink gets sucked into it.

The skin has multiple layers. The outer layer of skin is called the epidermis. It sheds hundreds of thousands of dead skin cells every day. Tattoo art would not last long on this layer. So tattoo artists place ink into the second layer of skin. This is known as the dermis. The body treats the ink as foreign particles. It sends white blood cells called macrophages to absorb and

PARTS OF THE SKIN

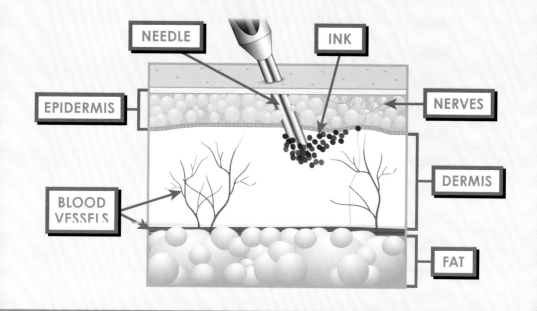

NEEDLE

INK

EPIDERMIS

NERVES

BLOOD VESSELS

DERMIS

FAT

Tattoo artists must push ink into the dermis.

destroy the ink. This is the same way the

body fights bacteria and viruses. But the ink

particles are too big for the macrophages

to destroy. So they keep the ink suspended

in place. When the macrophages die,

they release the ink particles. The ink is

absorbed by other macrophages. The cycle begins again.

A PAINFUL PROCESS

The skin has many blood vessels. The tattoo needles puncture these. This causes mild bleeding. Tattoo artists frequently wipe

HEALTH RISKS

Getting a tattoo has a number of health risks. Tattoos are wounds, so there is always a risk of infection. There is also a risk of getting **blood-borne** diseases, such as hepatitis. People can also have allergic reactions to certain tattoo inks. Trained tattoo artists take steps to help prevent these issues. However, there is always a chance of complications. People experiencing problems should consult their doctors and tattoo artists.

away blood while tattooing someone. This way, they can see their work more clearly.

Tattooing is also painful. The skin has nerves. These send pain signals to the brain. Tattoo needles hit these nerves. People getting tattoo art experience moderate to severe pain. They often describe the pain as a burning sensation. It has also been compared to bee or wasp stings. "I always tell my clients to imagine a cat continuously scratching them with hot claws," says tattoo artist Anka Lavriv.[2] Tattooing is sometimes done without anesthetics. These are substances used

People have different pain tolerance levels. For some people, getting a tattoo can hurt a lot.

to dull pain. But some people use gels or

sprays to help numb the pain.

The severity of pain differs on different

areas of the body. Areas with lots of

nerve endings or thin skin are the most

painful. These include the rib cage, ankles, neck, and face. Areas with few nerve endings and with layers of fat and muscle are less painful. These include the upper arms, forearms, back, and thighs. The pain is often the worst at the beginning of a tattoo session. Eventually, the body begins releasing endorphins. These are chemicals that help relieve pain. They can make the pain more tolerable.

The fear of pain may stop some people from getting tattoo art. But some people, such as tattoo artist T. Phae Brangarrán, see it as a rite of passage. "The pain

People can talk with a tattoo artist to see where a certain tattoo might fit best on their bodies.

symbolizes death of the former self,

separating one from one's previous life.

When the procedure is complete, the

subject is now marked as one of the pierced or tattooed community," she wrote.[3]

Tattoo art can be placed on any part of the body with skin. This even includes the tongue. But the thickness and roughness of the skin in some places can make them

SCLERAL TATTOOING

People can tattoo their eyes. This is called scleral tattooing. The process is different from skin tattooing. Scleral tattooing involves injecting ink into the white, outer layer of the eye, called the sclera. This is done by using a syringe with a hollow needle at the end. It is known as a **hypodermic** needle. Scleral tattooing can cause major damage to the eye if not done properly. For this reason, many tattoo artists do not do it.

more difficult to tattoo. These include the palms of the hands and the soles of the feet. The skin in these areas also regrows more quickly than in other places. Tattoo art may not last as long there.

TYPES OF TATTOO ART

There are many different types of tattoo art. Blackwork only has solid black designs. Realism is a photo-realistic style. **Tribal** tattoos include elements from tribal cultures, such as different Polynesian or Native American cultures. 3D tattoos have shading and depth. This makes them look three-dimensional. The American traditional

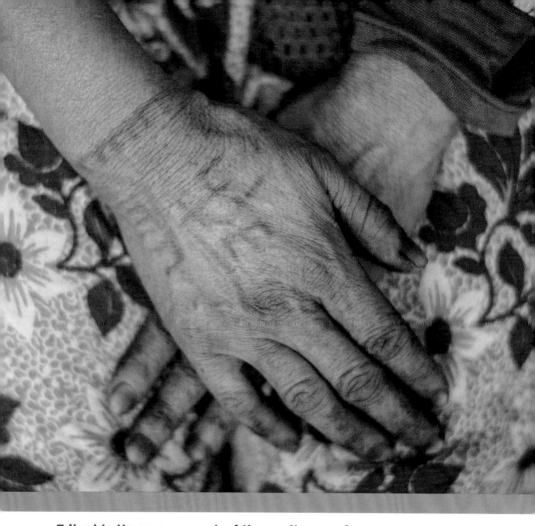

Tribal tattoos are part of the cultures of some Indigenous peoples in North Africa, such as the Amazigh.

style has clean, bold outlines. It is filled

with bright colors. It often features popular

designs from the 1950s and 1960s. These

include hearts, flowers, skulls, and anchors.

Some tattoos have their own unique names. Tattoos that cover all or most of the body are called bodysuits. Armbands are tattoos that encircle the upper arm or forearm. A sleeve tattoo is one that covers the arm from the wrist to the shoulder, or the leg from the ankle to the top of the thigh. Bodysuits and sleeves may be large tattoos. They may also be collections of smaller tattoos that have a common theme. Some people get numerous tattoos over the course of their lives. People with many tattoos are known as collectors. A body without tattoo art is sometimes referred to

Sometimes people need multiple sessions to finish a sleeve tattoo.

as a blank canvas. There are many forms

of tattoo art. People get tattoos for different

reasons. Big or small, tattoo art has a

lasting effect on those who get it.

CHAPTER TWO

WHAT IS THE HISTORY OF TATTOO ART?

In 1991, someone found a frozen human body in the mountains near the Italian and Austrian border in Europe. Scientists studied the body. They discovered it was approximately 5,300 years old. They named it Ötzi. The body had tattoos. They were the oldest ones ever discovered. No one

Ötzi was hidden by glacial ice for thousands of years.

knows how far back tattooing goes. Some

scientists believe it may go back much

further than Ötzi's time.

Ötzi's tattoos were simple. They

consisted of rows of lines and crosses.

They were located on his wrist, lower back,

The British Museum has many ancient artifacts.

and lower legs. The scientists who studied
him discovered that he had health problems
in those areas. They suggested that the
tattoos may not have been art. They may
have been a form of medical treatment
used to relieve pain.

In 2018, experts looked at a mummy on display in the British Museum. The mummy was around 5,000 years old. The experts noticed markings on its arm. They realized the markings were of a bull and a sheep. Scientist Daniel Antoine called it "the earliest use of figurative tattoos."[4] That means the tattoos represented real objects. Unlike Ötzi's tattoos, these may have been purely decorative. They may be the earliest examples of tattoo art.

TATTOO ART AROUND THE WORLD

Tattooing has been done in many different parts of the world throughout history.

The peoples of the Polynesian islands began tattooing thousands of years ago. These islands are spread across the southern Pacific Ocean. The Samoan, Tongan, and Maori peoples developed distinct styles. They consist of solid black geometric patterns and spirals. Some patterns represent family histories. Others show social rank. Some are thought to protect people from evil or harm.

Some Native American Nations in North America practice tattooing. Among these are Inuit and Iroquois peoples. Tattooing was also done by some ancient people

Inuit tattoo artist Hovak Johnston is trying to revive her culture's traditional tattooing methods.

of Peru in South America and the Mayan people of Southern Mexico and Central America. Tattoo art among these cultures often included geometric designs and images of animals.

Tattooing was also common among some of China's tribal people, including the Dai people of Southern China. Both Dai men and women wore tattoo art. They even tattooed children. Some were as young as five years old. Some Dai people today have tattoo art too.

Chinese visitors in Japan recorded seeing tattoo art there in the 200s CE. Tattoo art in Japan reached its peak between the 1600s and the early 1800s. According to art historian Kelly Richman-Abdou, this was due "to the prevalence of the colorful and pictorial Ukiyo-e woodblock print."[5]

Many Japanese tattoos feature cultural symbols and have a lot of details.

This was a type of art popular in Japan at the time. It was recreated as tattoo art by both upper- and lower-class people. But tattoo art was banned in Japan in 1872. It had become linked with lower-class people and criminals. Tattoo artists continued to tattoo people in secret. The ban was lifted in 1948. But many Japanese people still do not approve of tattoo art.

EUROPE AND THE UNITED STATES

Tattooing has been done in Europe since the time of Ötzi. The Picts lived in Scotland until the mid-800s CE. They tattooed images of animals onto their bodies. The ancient Romans used tattoos to identify criminals and enslaved people as early as the 600s BCE.

Many Europeans traveled to Palestine in the Middle East during the Middle Ages (500 to 1400–1500 CE). Palestine was

Today, people continue to get tattoos of animals. Sometimes the tattoos are images of their pets.

also known as the Holy Land. Some people

went there on **pilgrimages** to religious

sites. Others went there to fight in wars.

Some of them had crosses tattooed on

their bodies. This was a sign that they

had been to the Holy Land. The Razzouk

family lives in Jerusalem, Israel, which was once part of Palestine. The family has been tattooing pilgrims for 700 years. Wassim Razzouk is a tattoo artist. He said in a 2018 interview, "For a lot of pilgrims, their visit to the Holy Land changes them in a way and leaves a mark on their soul, so that they want to leave a mark on their body as well."[6]

In the 1700s, British and American sailors began visiting islands in the South Pacific. Some sailors were tattooed by the people there. In time, some sailors became tattoo artists. They tattooed other sailors aboard their ships. Some also worked as

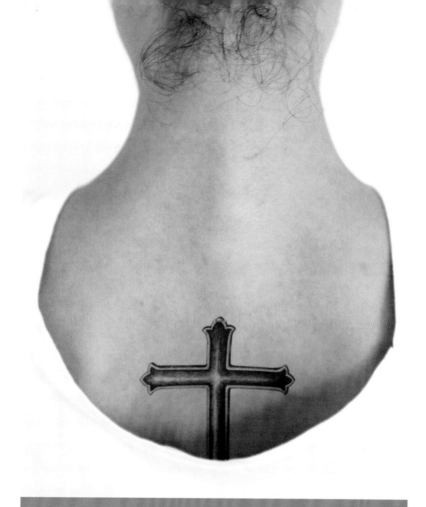

Some people's tattoos are symbols of religious faith.

tattoo artists in port cities, such as New

York City. They often used maritime images

in tattoo art. These included ships, anchors,

and mermaids.

Martin Hildebrandt was a tattoo artist in New York City. He opened the city's first tattoo businesses in the late 1800s. He tattooed sailors and soldiers. He also tattooed circus performers. Tattoo art became popular with circus performers in

SAILOR JERRY

Norman Collins was a tattoo artist. He served in the US Navy starting in the 1920s. He tattooed his fellow sailors. People called him Sailor Jerry. Eventually he ran his own studio. Collins combined Japanese tattoo styles with American maritime imagery. His tattoo art had bold, black outlines and bright colors. It was popular with sailors. Today, it is known as the Sailor Jerry tattoo style. It is still popular in the United States.

Tattoo artist Edward Liberty tattoos a sailor in Boston, Massachusetts, in 1942.

the 1800s. Circuses hired people covered

with tattoo art. Circus goers would pay to

see them. Maud Wagner was a tattooed

circus performer in the early 1900s. She

later became a tattoo artist. She was

one of the first female tattoo artists in the

United States.

Tattoo art became more common during World War II (1939–1945). US flags and other patriotic symbols were popular. Tattoo art became a sign of strength and toughness after the war. It was also

OUTBREAK

New York City is known as the birthplace of modern tattooing in the United States. Many of the country's earliest tattoo artists worked there. The city suffered an outbreak of hepatitis B in the late 1950s. Hepatitis B is a virus. People can get it when blood from an infected person enters their bodies. It made many people sick. Health officials blamed the outbreak on tattoo studios. In 1961, tattooing was banned in the city. It didn't become legal again until 1997.

embraced by gang members and criminals. Over time, people began associating tattoo art with outlaws. This made it **taboo**. But it became popular again in the 1970s and 1980s. People began seeing tattoo art as a form of rebellion. Famous entertainers got tattoo art. People saw it on TV and in movies. This influenced how they viewed tattoo art. Many people began to get it. By the 1990s, tattoo art had become more socially acceptable. In 2019, approximately 25 percent of people in the United States had tattoo art.

TATTOOING METHODS

The way tattoo art was made changed over time. The earliest method may have involved cutting a person's skin with a sharp object and then rubbing pigment into it. Tools were later made specifically for tattooing. In 1985, an ancient set of tattooing tools was discovered in Tennessee. The set included bone needles and shells for holding pigments. Scientists estimated the tools were around 3,600 years old. Other ancient bone tattooing tools have been found on the Polynesian islands. Bronze tools have been found at ancient sites in

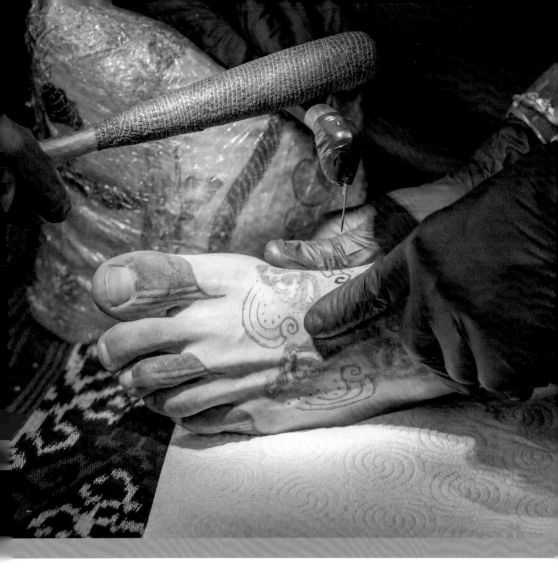

Traditional ways of tattooing, such as the tapping method, are still used in some places today.

Egypt. These tools were dipped in ink.

They were used to poke the ink into the

skin. This is called the poking or pricking

method. Another common tool used around the world was a wood or bone handle with needles on one end. The needles were dipped in ink. A second wood or bone tool was used to tap the needles into the skin. This is called the tapping method.

The electric tattoo machine was made in the late 1800s. It had tattoo needles connected to a motor. The motor made the needles move up and down rapidly. Tattoo machines allowed people to make tattoo art much faster. They revolutionized the tattoo industry.

Tattoo machines evolved over time. Today, they are very efficient tools.

CHAPTER THREE

HOW IS TATTOO ART MADE TODAY?

Today, most tattooing is done in tattoo studios. The studios are also called tattoo parlors or shops. Tattoo studios have tables and chairs for clients to sit or lie on while they get tattooed. These places have equipment for **sterilizing** tools. The walls are often covered with

Some tattoo studios have art on the walls that people can draw inspiration from.

tattoo art. Some studios play music. It can help distract people from the pain of getting tattoos.

Most tattoo art is done by professional tattoo artists. They have trained with other artists. This is called an apprenticeship.

An apprenticeship can last from one to three years. Apprentices learn how to use a tattoo machine. Or they may learn to use traditional tools. They also learn how to tattoo safely. A college degree is not needed to be a tattoo artist. But some people get college degrees in art. Some schools offer tattoo programs. The Master

TRADITIONAL TATTOOING

Not all tattoo artists use tattoo machines. Some still use traditional tools and methods. The tapping and poking methods are used by some artists. Some still use tools made of wood or bone. Artists use these methods and tools as ways to connect with the past. Others use them to honor cultural traditions.

Tattoo Institute is a tattoo school in Florida. It is the only tattoo school recognized by the US Department of Education.

Tattoo artists spend many hours practicing. Some practice on fruits, such as oranges and bananas. Others practice on themselves. They make mistakes during this time. Their lines may not be straight. Their tattooing may be too deep. That can make tattoo art look foggy. This is called a blowout. Tattoo artist Laura Martinez discussed tattooing in a 2019 interview. She said, "It's really hard to accept and face your own mistake, especially when it's on someone's body forever. I personally had nightmares about it in the beginning."[7]

A license is sometimes required to work as a tattoo artist. Certain requirements must be met to get a license. A set number of training hours are needed. First aid and CPR training are often necessary. CPR training can be helpful if a client passes out and stops breathing. Training in blood-borne diseases may be required.

TATTOO PREP

For those getting a tattoo, choosing a design is the first step. Some people know what they want before they go to a tattoo

Flash designs can include flowers, skulls, lettering, arm and ankle bands, and much more.

studio. Others might not. Most tattoo

studios have books containing artwork.

People can choose designs from the books.

This stock art is called flash. Some people

provide their own designs. Some tattoo

artists create custom artwork for clients.

A lot happens before tattooing begins. The artist must check the client's age. A person must be at least eighteen to get a tattoo in the United States. A person can be younger in some states if a parent is with him or her. The client often has to sign a waiver. It explains the health risks of tattooing. The client agrees to accept the risks when he or she signs it.

Next, the tools and work space are prepared. Some tattoo artists cover their tattoo machines with plastic. It protects them from body fluids and ink. They might cover the tables and chairs with plastic

Artists dip the tip of their tattoo machines into ink to collect the substance. Then, they insert the ink into the skin.

as well. They also put on plastic gloves.

This helps prevent the spread of bacteria.

Then the inks and needle are brought

out. Inks are poured from bottles into

small plastic cups. A needle is removed

from its sterile wrapper. It is attached to a tattoo machine.

Lastly, the client's skin is prepared. The skin where the tattoo will go is cleaned. Any hair at the spot is removed with a shaving razor. This makes the skin easier to see. Then the tattoo design is transferred to the skin. This is often done using stencils. Stencils are made with special transfer paper. Designs can be hand drawn onto the paper. Or they can be printed on it using a copy machine. The paper is carefully placed on the skin. The ink sticks to the skin when the paper is peeled off. It serves as a

Tattoo artists keep the stencil on a person's skin for just one or two minutes.

pattern. It also gives the client a preview of

what the tattoo will look like. The client can

suggest changes before tattooing begins.

Stencils aren't always used. Designs can

be drawn on the skin by hand. Some tattoo

artists use both methods. They begin with a stencil. Then they draw details by hand.

GETTING A TATTOO

Tattoo art is mostly done using a tattoo machine. The machine has a needle on one end. The other end has a motor that makes the needle move up and down. The speed can be changed. The needle can move between fifty and three thousand times per minute. Different speeds are used for different techniques. Shading uses slower speeds. Linework uses faster speeds.

There are many different types of needles. Some have a single point.

Artists use different needles based on the designs clients want.

But most have several. The points are

arranged in different ways. Each type of

needle is used for a different job. Some

needles have points arranged together

in tight circles. They are used for making

narrow lines. Others have points spaced

farther apart. They are used for filling in

large spaces. Ink is applied to the needle by dipping it in a cup of ink. The needle runs out of ink quickly. It has to be dipped in ink every few seconds. The tattoo machine is controlled with a foot pedal. This keeps the artist's hands free. The machine is held in one hand. The other hand pulls the client's skin taut. This makes the surface of the skin flat. A flat surface is easier to work on. The free hand is also used to wipe away blood and excess ink from the skin. This makes the skin easier to see.

Tattoo art is made in stages. The first stage is called outlining. The tattoo machine

Tattoo artists have to concentrate while working. They want to make sure their clients get the best designs possible.

is used to trace the outline of the pattern.

Some tattoo art has shading. It is usually done after outlining. Shading is color that fades from dark to light. More ink is applied to the dark areas than the light areas. Shading gives tattoo art depth. But not all tattoo art has shading. Some have areas with solid colors. Coloring is the final stage. Solid colors are made by applying ink evenly over an area. Tattoo art often has more than one color. The tattoo needle is cleaned each time a new color is used. This keeps the colors from mixing.

Small tattoos can take as little as twenty minutes to make. But large ones can take many hours. Artists often take breaks during tattoo sessions. This gives them a chance to rest their hands. It also gives their clients a break from the pain. Tattoo art is not always made in one session. Large art is often done in two or more sessions.

Long sessions can be too painful for some

people. The skin may also need time to heal

before more work can be done on it.

AFTERCARE

Tattooing leaves open wounds in the skin.

The wounds need to be treated to ensure

FADING ART

Tattoo art fades over time. Ultraviolet light from the sun causes the ink to break down. Friction may also make tattoos fade. Friction is caused by clothing rubbing against the skin. Ink quality also affects fading. Poor-quality inks often fade faster than high-quality inks. Tattoo artists can retouch faded tattoo art. Fresh ink can make it look new again.

they heal properly. This treatment is called aftercare. Aftercare begins as soon as the tattooing session is finished. First, the skin is cleaned. Then moisturizer is added to the tattooed skin. This helps with any itching. The skin is covered with a bandage or with plastic wrap. This helps keep out dirt and bacteria.

Tattoo art can take two to three weeks to fully heal. People must perform their own aftercare during that time. Tattoo artists teach their clients what to do at home. Following their instructions is important to prevent infections or other health issues.

Artists will tell clients when they can take off their wrappings.

Dan Hunter is the owner of Authority Tattoo.
He writes: "Post-tattoo care should not be
taken lightly—you need to know how to take
care of a tattoo as best as possible. Failing
to follow your tattoo artist's advice could
lead to damaging consequences."[8]

CHAPTER FOUR

WHAT IS THE CULTURAL IMPACT OF TATTOO ART?

Tattoo art impacts cultures in many ways. It is often seen in the media and entertainment industry. Tattoo art is shown in movies and TV shows. There have even been shows dedicated to tattoo art, such as *Miami Ink* and *Ink Master.* There are many

For many people, getting a tattoo is a way to express themselves.

tattoo magazines, such as *Tattoo* and *Inked*.

The internet has helped tattoo art gain

recognition. Many websites show off tattoo

art. Tattoo studios often have websites to

help bring in customers. Artists use social

media sites, such as Facebook, to connect with people.

Celebrities have helped make tattoo art socially acceptable. Many famous actors and musicians have tattoo art. They include Lady Gaga, Justin Bieber, and Rihanna. Even some politicians have tattoo art. Canadian prime minister Justin Trudeau and New Zealand foreign minister Nanaia Mahuta have tattoos.

Kids can get involved in tattoo art too. Some stores sell rub-on tattoos for kids. The art is rubbed onto the skin. It wears off in a few days. In 2006, Phil Padwe wrote a book called *Mommy Has a Tattoo*. It has characters with tattoo art. The book teaches lessons about accepting people who may look different. In 2009, a toy

Tattoo stickers come in many designs, such as butterflies, unicorns, dinosaurs, pirates, superheroes, and much more.

company released a doll. It came with

tattoo stickers. Kids could place the stickers

on the doll's body. These items may help

children view tattoo art as commonplace.

DIFFERENT VIEWS

Not everyone views tattoo art the same

way. Some people do not approve of it.

People have associated tattooing with gangs and criminals for many years. This still affects how individuals with tattoos are seen. People may see them as gang members or drug users. They may see them as uneducated. This is called stereotyping. Stereotyping is judging a group of people based on a few members. It is one reason tattoo art is not more widely accepted today.

Some have religious reasons for not getting tattoos. Some Christians believe that tattooing is a sin. Tattooing is forbidden in the Islamic and Jewish faiths.

Negative views of tattoo art affect peoples' lives. Some businesses want employees to cover their tattoo art with clothing. The US military restricts the types of tattoos soldiers and sailors can get. People with visible tattoos are banned from some public areas in Japan.

CULTURAL APPROPRIATION

Cultural appropriation is when people adopt aspects of a culture that is not their own. It is not seen as socially acceptable. People sometimes use images from different cultures as tattoo art. Some people may not belong to those cultures. They may like the images. But they may not know the history and meaning of them. This can be cultural appropriation.

Some employers want people to cover up their tattoos, but others are fine with this form of expression.

THE FUTURE OF TATTOO ART

Tattoo art has changed over many years and continues to do so. Designs are becoming more complex. Scientists and engineers are making advances in tattoo technology. Changes include inks that glow in the dark. There are also inks that interact with the environment. Temperature and light can make them change colors.

Technology has made it easier to design tattoo art. People can design tattoos on computers and tablets. Maxime Etienne is a tattoo artist. He says, "Using an iPad makes it much easier to make changes to a client's design. Before the iPad, we would have to sketch our ideas on paper, and if the client didn't like it, we'd have to start from scratch."[9]

Many people are interested in tattoo art. They may view it as a way to express

Many people enjoy having tattoo art.

themselves. Tattoo art is part of many

cultures around the world. It has been

around for thousands of years. It continues

to grow and evolve.

GLOSSARY

blood-borne

carried or passed by blood

cultures

the shared behaviors, beliefs, and customs of groups of people

hypodermic

made to be used under the skin

pigments

substances that put colors into other materials

pilgrimages

journeys to sacred places

sterilizing

removing all microbes

taboo

something a society deems improper

tribal

relating to Indigenous peoples

SOURCE NOTES

INTRODUCTION: A HUMAN CANVAS

1. Quoted in Carmen Nyssen, "Language of Tatau, Ta Tatau, Tattoo," *Buzzworthy Tattoo*, June 10, 2020. www.buzzworthytattoo.com.

CHAPTER ONE: WHAT IS TATTOO ART?

2. Quoted in Rosemary Donahue, "How Much Does Getting a Tattoo Hurt? The Experts Weigh in," *Allure*, June 24, 2018. www.allure.com.

3. T. Phae Drangarrán, "Body Modification and Contemporary American Rites of Passage," *Art and Discord Studios*, September 23, 2019. www.artanddiscordstudios.com.

CHAPTER TWO: WHAT IS THE HISTORY OF TATTOO ART?

4. Quoted in Felix Allen, "World's Oldest Tattoo Found on 5,000-Year-Old Mummy," *New York Post*, March 1, 2018. https://nypost.com.

5. Kelly Richman-Abdou, "Irezumi: Exploring the Ancient Techniques and Evolution of Traditional Japanese Tattoos," *My Modern Met*, July 30, 2019. https://mymodernmet.com.

6. Quoted in Derek Stoffel, "Christian Pilgrims Flock to Storied 700-Year-Old Jerusalem Tattoo Parlour," *CBC*, July 19, 2018. www.cbc.ca.

CHAPTER THREE: HOW IS TATTOO ART MADE TODAY?

7. Quoted in Arielle Pardes and Hannah Malach, "16 Things I Wish I Knew Before I Became a Tattoo Artist," *Cosmopolitan*, December 11, 2019. www.cosmopolitan.com.

8. Dan Hunter, "Tattoo Aftercare: How to Care for a New Tattoo," *Authority Tattoo*, July 9, 2017. https://authoritytattoo.com.

CHAPTER FOUR: WHAT IS THE CULTURAL IMPACT OF TATTOO ART?

9. Quoted in Max Langridge, "How Technology Will Change Your Next Tattoo, According to the Experts," *Dmarge*, January 30, 2020. www.dmarge.com.

FOR FURTHER RESEARCH

BOOKS

Nicholas Faulkner, *The History of Tattoos and Body Modification*. New York: Rosen Publishing, 2019.

Nicholas Faulkner and Frank Spalding, *Tattoo Removal*. New York: Rosen Publishing, 2019.

Hal Marcovitz, *The Art of Tattoo*. San Diego: ReferencePoint Press, 2020.

INTERNET SOURCES

Rachel Feltman, "Tattoos Are Permanent, but the Science Behind Them Just Shifted," *Popular Science*, March 6, 2018. www.popsci.com.

"A Revolution in Tattooing," *Smithsonian*, August 20, 2020. www.si.edu.

"What Is the History of Tattoos?" *McGill University*, March 20, 2017. www.mcgill.ca.

WEBSITES

Authority Tattoo
https://authoritytattoo.com

Authority Tattoo provides well researched and medically reviewed information on tattooing.

Master Tattoo Institute
www.mastertattooinstitute.com

The Master Tattoo Institute is a licensed tattoo school located in Florida.

Mayo Clinic
www.mayoclinic.org

Mayo Clinic provides medical care and resources to people across the United States. It also has useful information on tattoo health risks.

INDEX

IMAGE CREDITS

ABOUT THE AUTHOR

Ryan Gale is an artist and writer from Minnesota. He got his first tattoo art at the age of eighteen.